Bulldogs look mean but love to snuggle

Bulldogs

Joy Frisch

A+

Smart Apple Media

COPYRIGHT

🐏 Published by Smart Apple Media

1980 Lookout Drive, North Mankato, MN 56003

Designed by Rita Marshall

Copyright © 2004 Smart Apple Media. International copyright reserved in

all countries. No part of this book may be reproduced in any form without

written permission from the publisher.

Printed in the United States of America

🐏 Photographs by Accent Alaska.com (Ken Graham), Barbara Augello, Norvia

Behling, Corbis (Hulton-Deutsch Collection, Sygma), dogpix.com (Larry

Reynolds), Unicorn Stock Photos (Ken Schwab), Dolly Van Zaane

🐏 Library of Congress Cataloging-in-Publication Data

Frisch, Joy. Bulldogs / by Joy Frisch.

p. cm. – (Dog breeds) Summary: Introduces the physical characteristics,

life cycle, breeding, training, and care of bulldogs. Includes instructions for an

activity involving drawing.

🐏 ISBN 1-58340-316-7

1. Bulldog–Juvenile literature. [1. Bulldog. 2. Dogs.] I. Title. II. Series.

SF429.B85F58 2003   636.72–dc21   2002042812

🐏 First Edition 9 8 7 6 5 4 3 2 1

Bulldogs

A Powerhouse Dog

No other dog looks as grumpy or dangerous as the bulldog. But how this dog looks is much different than how it acts. The bulldog may look ready to fight, but it is actually a gentle, quiet dog. The English bulldog is considered the original bulldog, but there are other kinds of bulldogs, too. Two of the more common are the French bulldog and the American bulldog. The French bulldog is small and easy to recognize by its bat-like ears. The American bulldog is larger

French bulldogs have stiff, bat-like ears

than the English bulldog. All bulldogs have wide, stocky

bodies with sturdy legs and short tails. Tails can be either

straight or curled. Bulldogs' short, smooth coats can be

white, red, tan, streaked, or patched. **An American bulldog named Petey starred in the 1994 movie *The Little Rascals*.**

English bulldogs are especially powerful.

They stand 12 to 14 inches (31–36 cm) tall

from the ground to the tops of their

shoulders and weigh between 40 and 50 pounds (18–23 kg).

Most of their weight comes from muscle. Most famous for

Petey, the pet bulldog of the Little Rascals gang

Bulldog pups grow quickly into strong, sturdy dogs

their large heads and droopy mouths, bulldogs have short,

flat noses and lots of loose skin that hangs below their jaws.

These folds of skin are called jowls. Bulldogs' ears are small

and folded.

A Bulldog's Life

Female bulldogs are pregnant for nine weeks before

whelping, or giving birth. Whelping can be dangerous for a

bulldog mother and her puppies. Because of their large size,

the puppies' heads can get stuck and cause problems.

Sometimes, a **veterinarian** will have to perform an operation

to deliver the puppies. Bulldogs usually have **litters** of 6 to 15

puppies. When they are born, bulldog puppies are small

enough to fit in a person's hand. Their eyes open after 10 days.

A litter of English bulldog puppies

Young puppies make squeaking sounds when they are hungry.

They must stay with their mother for six weeks before they are

weaned. Bulldog puppies like to play and wrestle with one

another. By the time they are one year **Bulldogs should**
not go into

old, they are full-grown. Bulldogs may **deep water to**
cool off in hot

have more health problems than other **weather**
because they

kinds of dogs. Their short muzzles **cannot swim.**

sometimes cause breathing problems. Bulldogs may snort,

sneeze, or even snore! With good care, though, a bulldog can

live up to 10 years.

The Fighting Bulldog

Long ago, bulldogs were used as farm dogs. They protected farmers from dangerous bulls. This is how bulldogs

Growing bulldogs like to wrestle with one another

got their name. When people saw their bravery, they decided to train bulldogs to fight. The bulldog **breed** developed in Great Britain around 1200 and was used for a sport called bullbaiting. In a fight, a bull would be tied to a short rope. A bulldog would jump and bite the bull's nose. The bulldog that could hang on the longest would win. Sometimes the dogs were tossed or injured by the bull's horns. Many bulldogs were killed. Bulldogs were also

The bulldog is the national symbol of Great Britain. The British believe it represents strength and stubbornness.

Bullbaiting was a dangerous, cruel sport

used to fight lions, monkeys, and bears. Bullbaiting and

other bulldog fighting sports were outlawed in Great Britain in

1835. After that, few people wanted bulldogs because the dogs

were mean and dangerous. However, some people wanted to

save the bulldog, so they carefully raised the dogs to be gentle.

A Loyal Companion

Today, most bulldogs in North America are family pets.

They are sweet and loving dogs. They are good with children

and protective of them. Bulldogs are not very active dogs,

but they still need exercise. Because of their heavy bodies,

bulldogs do not run well. In fact, jogging can hurt their legs.

Short walks are best. Bulldogs can become overweight if they

do not get enough exercise. It can cost a lot of money to

Regular exercise helps keep a bulldog healthy

have a bulldog for a pet. Because many puppies die young,

bulldogs can be hard to find. This makes them expensive. The

special health needs of a bulldog can also add up in veterinar-

ian bills. Despite the cost of owning a **The deep wrinkles on a bulldog's face need to be cleaned daily to prevent infection.**

bulldog, many people think the bulldog is a

wonderful pet. It has come a long way from

its fighting past. Today's bulldog is a loyal and

loving dog that enjoys being part of a family.

A bulldog's wrinkles deepen as it gets older

A Fighter's Body

Even though bulldogs no longer fight, they still have the strong body of a fighter. This activity will help you see what makes a bulldog's body so different from other dogs' bodies.

What You Need

A pencil

Paper

Pictures of bulldogs

Pictures of other breeds of dogs, such as retrievers, poodles, or collies

What You Do

1. Look at the bulldog pictures.

2. Draw a picture of a bulldog's body. Then, draw a close-up of a bulldog's face.

3. Make a list of the body parts that would help make the bulldog a good fighter.

4. Look at the pictures of other kinds of dogs. What makes bulldogs different from other dogs? Compare their legs and heads. Compare their paws and teeth. What do you like best about bulldogs?

A bulldog's body is packed with muscles

Index

Words to Know

breed (BREED)—a type of dog, such as a poodle, collie, or bulldog

litters (LITT-urz)—groups of puppies born at the same time

muzzles (MUZ-elz)—the parts of dogs' faces that stick forward, including the nose, mouth, and jaws

veterinarian (VET-ur-eh-NAIR-ee-en)—a doctor for animals

weaned (WEEND)—when a puppy stops drinking its mother's milk and starts eating other foods

Read More

Alderton, David. *Dogs*. New York: Dorling Kindersley, 1993.

Wilcox, Charlotte. *The Bulldog*. Mankato, Minn.: Capstone Press, 1999.

Williams, Hank, and Carol Williams. *A New Owner's Guide to Bulldogs*. Neptune City, N.J.: T.F.H. Publications, 1998.

Internet Sites

American Kennel Club: Bulldog
http://www.akc.org/breeds/recbreeds/bulld.cfm

The Bulldog Club of America
http://www.thebca.org

Fact Monster Pets
http://www.factmonster.com/pets.html

The Quality Bulldog Magazine
http://bulldogsmonthly.com

INFORMATION